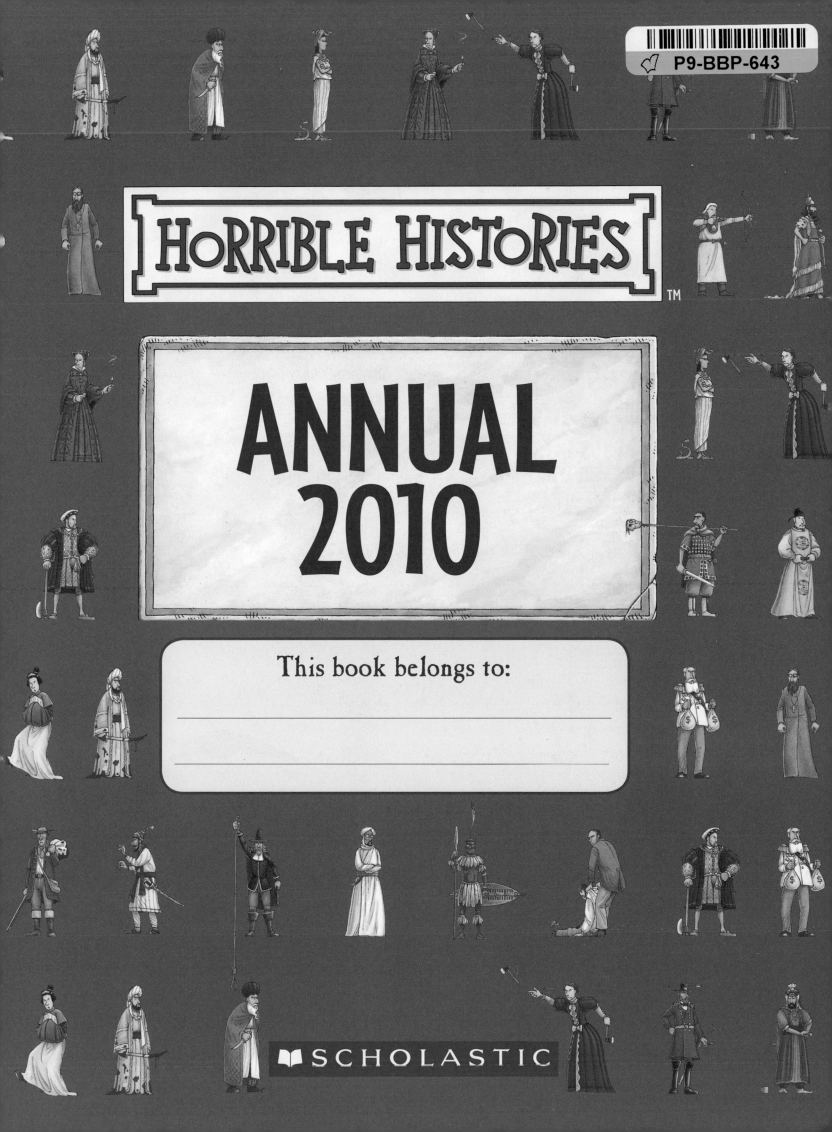

# HORRIBLE HISTORIES™

## ANNUAL 2010

This book belongs to:

_____

_____

SCHOLASTIC

# Contents

# Acropolis Now!

Our historical journey around the world starts with swords and sandals in ancient Greece.

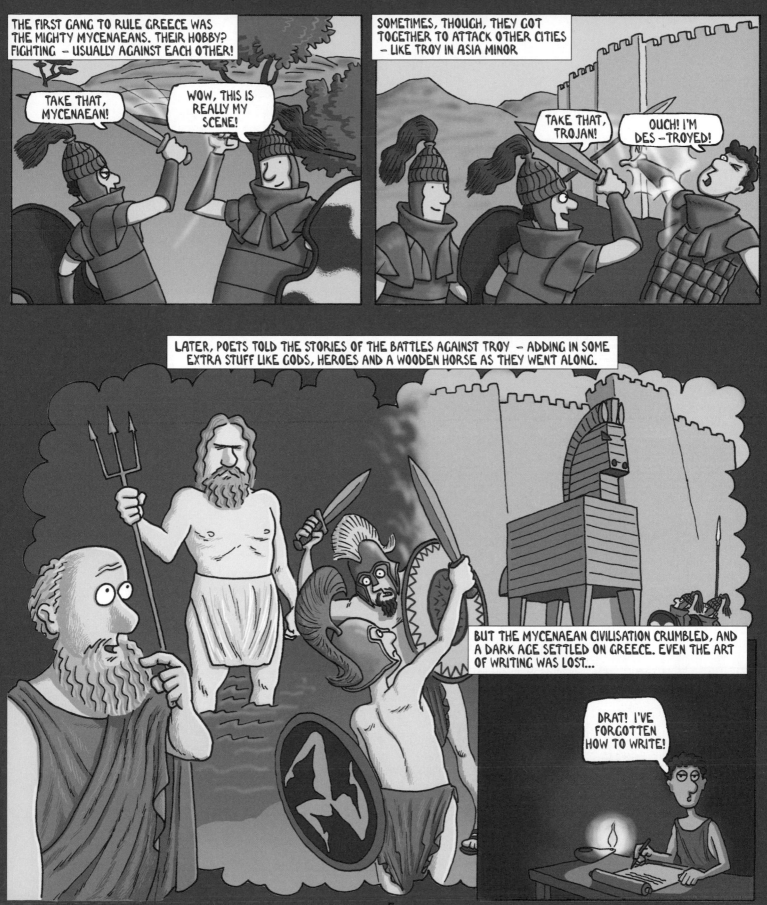

THE FIRST GANG TO RULE GREECE WAS THE MIGHTY MYCENAEANS. THEIR HOBBY? FIGHTING – USUALLY AGAINST EACH OTHER!

TAKE THAT, MYCENAEAN!

WOW, THIS IS REALLY MY SCENE!

SOMETIMES, THOUGH, THEY GOT TOGETHER TO ATTACK OTHER CITIES – LIKE TROY IN ASIA MINOR

TAKE THAT, TROJAN!

OUCH! I'M DES –TROYED!

LATER, POETS TOLD THE STORIES OF THE BATTLES AGAINST TROY – ADDING IN SOME EXTRA STUFF LIKE GODS, HEROES AND A WOODEN HORSE AS THEY WENT ALONG.

BUT THE MYCENAEAN CIVILISATION CRUMBLED, AND A DARK AGE SETTLED ON GREECE. EVEN THE ART OF WRITING WAS LOST...

DRAT! I'VE FORGOTTEN HOW TO WRITE!

# Thermopylae

When the Persian king Xerxes invaded Greece with his huge army, he was expecting the Greeks to be pushovers. But in a narrow pass called Thermopylae he ran into a small force of Spartans – Greece's toughest (and barmiest!) warriors.

## AWFUL AMBUSH

At first the Spartans were winning the battle. The Persians kept attacking the Greeks... and kept getting chopped to bits. King Xerxes was hopping mad.

But his fortunes changed when a sneaky Greek traitor showed the Persians a secret path through the mountains. They used this to creep up behind the Spartans.

When the Spartan king, Leonidas, saw that his men were going to be bashed from behind, he told them to leg it. But he and his bodyguards stayed put, 'cos there was nothing a Spartan liked better than getting killed in battle. Leo and his men got surrounded, but they refused to surrender – even when the Persians pincushioned them with arrows!

King Xerxes is definitely not pleased with the way things are going.

Spot the slimy traitor! What a secret-route-revealing rotter!

Some of the Persians make a big splash in the battle as they get shoved off the cliff by the Greeks!

Battily brave King Leonidas and his bodyguards are ready to fight to the death.

OH, NOT BAD PARON... CAN'T COMPLAIN

The Spartans stay cool as cucumbers. They spend their whole lives in tough training, so being in battle must be a picnic by comparison.

Some smooth Spartans pass the time by combing their hair and oiling their bodies. (You've got to look your best – even when you are facing certain death!)

This Spartan has really got himself into hot water. He's having a sneaky soak in Thermopylae's famous hot springs. The name Thermopylae actually means 'hot gates'.

# Think Like a Greek

One thing the Greeks had in abundance was new ideas. Great ones, bad ones, wacky ones, super scientific or superstitious rot – they had the loopy lot.

The Greeks had some of the cleverest and craziest thinkers of ancient times. Take just two of them – Socrates (a philosopher) and Pythagoras (a kind of cranky maths teacher – see box on the right).

## Ask to annoy

Socrates invented his own type of questioning – the 'Socratic Method'. His trick was to find a person who thought they were really wise, then ask them lots of difficult and annoying questions until they finally shouted, 'I don't KNOW!' and stormed off. Why not try this groovy Greek trick on your teacher?

Socrates was always hanging around with young people, telling them not to believe in the old gods. In Athens this was punishable by death. Socrates was ordered to drink poison. (Getting your smartest thinker to kill himself – now that is stupid.)

## Strange superstitions

Potty Pythagoras' followers weren't the only ones with strange beliefs. The Greeks were very superstitious people. They believed that…

---

## PY'S POTTY PUPILS

The pupils of Pythagoras lived apart from the rest of the Greeks and had some batty rules.
1. Don't eat beans. They believed these contained the souls of the dead.
(Plus they gave you wind – which ruined your concentration when you were doing some particular tricky maths.)
2. Never wear clothes that have knots in them.
3. Don't touch the fire with an iron poker.
4. Don't touch a white cockerel.
5. Don't eat the heart of an animal.
6. Don't stand on your fingernail clippings.
7. Don't leave the mark of your body on a bed when you get up. Smooth it out!
8. Don't look in a mirror beside a lamp.
9. Help a man to load something – but never help him unload.

---

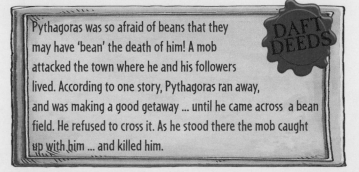

Pythagoras was so afraid of beans that they may have 'bean' the death of him! A mob attacked the town where he and his followers lived. According to one story, Pythagoras ran away, and was making a good getaway … until he came across a bean field. He refused to cross it. As he stood there the mob caught up with him … and killed him.

DAFT DEEDS

• Birds were messengers between earth and heaven,   and the moon was a resting place for spirits on their way to heaven.

• Hecate, goddess of witchcraft and crossroads appeared at crossroads on clear nights, along with ghosts and howling phantom dogs. The Greeks left food at crossroads for her. (She was also asked for help with curing madness – the Greeks believed madness was caused by the spirits of the dead.)

WHAT?! NO DOG FOOD?

• They could read the future in the guts of dead birds.

WHAT DO THEY SAY?

IN THE FUTURE THERE WILL BE FEWER BIRDS

• They also thought there were spirits called 'daimons' around. Some were good and protected you; some were evil and could lead you into wickedness. Even supposedly clever people like Socrates believed in daimons.

But some Greek ideas weren't quite so bonkers.

IT WASN'T ME SIR, IT WAS MY DAIMON

## Dreadful Democracy

Many countries today are run as democracies. That means every adult has a vote on who gets to be in the government.

Athens, being really groovy, had the first democracy. But because they didn't think everyone was equal, they didn't get it quite right...

EVERYBODY HAS A VOTE

HOORAY!

GROOVY

... EXCEPT WOMEN OF COURSE

HOORAY!

GROOVY

NO SLAVES WILL HAVE THE VOTE OF COURSE

HOORAY!

GROOVY

NO POOR PEOPLE OF COURSE

HOORAY!

GROOVY

AND NO ONE UNDER THE AGE OF THIRTY OF COURSE!

HOORAY!

GROOVY

OTHERWISE ... EVERYBODY HAS A VOTE!

GROOVY

# Some Great Greek Brain Pain

## WARRIOR WATCH

Look carefully at these two pictures of Greek 'hoplite' warriors arguing about who's got the best helmet. Both pictures show them in splendid uniforms, complete with multi-coloured horsehair crests... but there are a few differences. Are you eagle-eyed enough to spot all ten?

## Wicked Wordsearch

**Can you find the mythical characters listed below in this wordsquare?**

| U | S | H | M | F | N | T | O | S | P |
| W | Q | E | Y | R | E | L | N | G | I |
| S | Y | R | L | S | K | O | P | C | O |
| O | L | A | U | U | D | X | C | N | S |
| N | A | E | L | I | C | N | D | U | N |
| O | Z | T | E | D | V | R | E | F | T |
| R | P | S | H | O | T | S | E | R | O |
| C | O | Y | S | E | R | F | U | H | E |
| P | T | U | R | E | N | U | S | B | Z |
| Y | U | F | P | T | H | A | D | E | S |

| HERA | CRONOS |
|------|--------|
| ZEUS | ATHENA |
| HERCULES | HADES |
| POSEIDON | PERSEUS |

Which two are half-human?

## Questions of Sport

The only thing the Greeks liked better than war was sport! Can you answer these awesome Olympic questions?

I THINK I PREFER WAR, ACTUALLY...

1. In the Olympics, most athletes wore...
A. togas
B. kilts
C. nothing at all

2. Married women who sneaked into the games would be...

A. fined
B. thrown off the cliff
C. used as targets in the javelin events

3. At the Olympic Games, winners were given wreathes of...
A. olive leaves
B. lettuce leaves
C. celery

OI! SALAD-HEAD

4. Winners were also given extra awards when they got home, including...
A. medals
B. free meals
C. free haircuts

# Cactus If You Can

Let's jump from Greece to central America to dig up the Aztecs. THEY took the horriblest habits of petrifying peoples of the past and made them all their own. And if rivals tried to trick 'em, the Aztecs would lick 'em.

14

# Good Gore Guide

The Aztecs believed they had to give the Sun God
thousands of human lives. Why?

In Aztec legend, the sun was destroyed by a rain of blood and fire. The only way to make a new sun was for a god to set fire to himself. Nobody wanted the job – except Tecuciztecatl (say Te-koo-kiz-tekat-ill). The gods built a bonfire and invited Tec to jump in. He decided he was too busy. Then Nanahuatzin (say Nana-what-zin) took a long leap and landed in the fire. Pow! The earth had a sun. Tec jumped in too. Pow! There was another ball of light in the sky – Tec had become the moon.

## Sun stuck

Then, one by one the gods came to the feathered snake god, Quetzalcoatl, to have their hearts torn out ... and the sun began moving. The Aztecs said: "The gods gave their hearts to keep the sun moving – so should we!" And here's how they did it.

## How to have a heart, Aztec-style

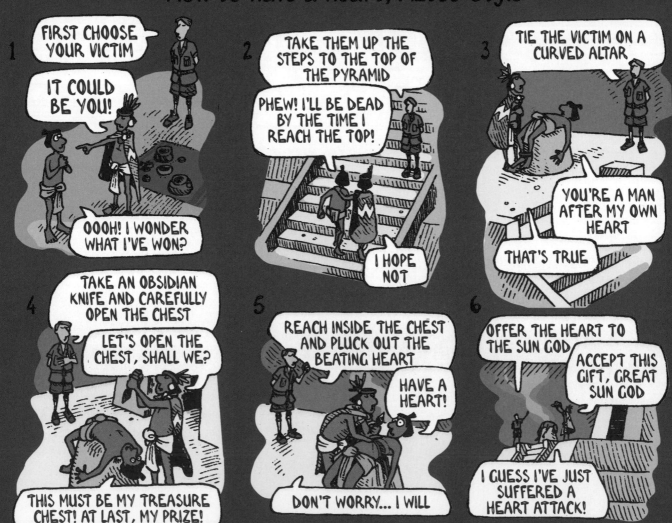

# WICKED WAYS TO GO

The Aztecs had four other main ways of sacrificing their victims – some crueller than others. What scary skull score would you give them?

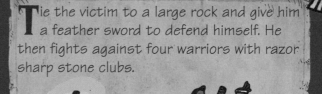

**C**ut off the head. This was usually the fate of female victims who'd spent some time acting as goddesses.

A quick way to go and you'd have had fun being treated as a goddess.

**T**ie the victim to a large rock and give him a feather sword to defend himself. He then fights against four warriors with razor sharp stone clubs.

You'd have to be a bird-brain to think those feathers would save you!

**T**ie the victim to poles, mark his heart with a white spot and shoot arrows at him. Don't aim at the spot at first – blood from the wounds makes the earth richer (apparently!).

It's no fun being a human pin-cushion.

**T**hrow the victim into a fire then pull him out. Repeat a few times. When he's lightly baked, do the heart sacrifice.

Nasty!

## Deadly daily

The Aztecs preferred sacrificing enemy warriors. The braver the enemy, the better the sacrifice. But they didn't just hack out hearts on special occasions, they did it all the time. They:
• sacrificed 20,000 in a single party when they opened the temple at Tenochtitlan
• had an army specially organised to keep the priests supplied with victims
• stirred up trouble among the conquered tribes so they had an excuse to go in and take prisoners to be sacrifice victims
• sacrificed 50,000 a year – that's a thousand a week, six an hour or one every ten minutes!

### Foul Facts

The worship of one gruesome god was particularly putrid. To honour Xipe Totec (Aztec for 'our flayed lord'), a priest skinned a man who had just been sacrificed – and wore his skin like a costume for at least 20 days, until it started rotting!

Aztec emperor Montezuma treated Spanish conquistador Hernan Cortés and his men as guests. Big mistake! After much bloodshed, the Aztecs booted the Spanish out, but they came back with local help. This time they weren't just dropping in for tadpoles and tortillas...

# Aztecs

Cortés got into a sticky situation – he got bonked on the head, and an Aztec tried to drag him off to be sacrificed. Luckily for him, a conquistador saved him by cutting off the Aztec's arm.

The Spanish started by burning and bashing the amazing city of Tenochtitlan. They wouldn't get invited back again – so they might as well knock it down!

AZ –TEC THAT!

The Spanish may have been mean, but their native allies were even meaner. They had suffered hundreds of years of cruelty under the Aztecs, and it was time for revenge.

# Attacked!

Conquistadors captured by the Aztecs were dragged up the great pyramid for a bit of open-heart surgery. Maybe the Aztecs wanted to see if the Spanish were really completely heartless!

The Aztecs were only used to cute little bite-sized pooches, so the Spanish soldiers' big vicious dogs were a nasty surprise in the backside!

Spanish soldiers took the chance to go for gold... the Aztecs' gold, that is. They went absolutely ape for it.

GIMME GOLD, GIMME GOLD, GIMME GOLD!

Razor-sharp Aztec swordclubs could slice off a head – but they bounced off Spanish steel armour.

The Aztecs' bravest warriors wore posh jaguar or eagle costumes – but fur and feathers were no good against blades and bullets.

# Some Heart-Chopping Challenges

## FURIOUS FIGHTERS

Aztec men loved to fight. When the war drum sounded every Aztec man was expected to pick up his weapons and join a group of 800 men. What other fantastic facts do you know about the Aztec warriors? Just answer True or False to the following...

1. Aztecs wore armour.
2. Aztec leaders were easy to spot because they wore large feather and reed structures on their shoulders.
3. Rich Aztec warriors wore gold and jewels when they went into battle.

DON'T YOU THINK THAT'S A LITTLE ... WELL ... TOO MUCH?

4. Aztecs believed in killing themselves rather than being captured.
5. The Aztec army needed to capture 20 enemy fighters for sacrifices – and NO less.

WHAT? ONLY 1?! GO BACK AND CONQUER THAT COUNTRY AGAIN!

6. Warriors short of food would would eat their dead friends.

HE WAS A GOOD WARRIOR, BUT HE WAS A GREAT BARBECUE!

## SAVAGE SPANISH

This poor Aztec's people have been attacked by conquistadors. He's so upset that he needs your help to unjumble some of his words.

They attacked my friend and cut off his MARS. They cut off his DEAH and it DROLLE across the ROLFO. Then they attacked the others, stabbing them, SPAREING them and striking them with their DROWSS. They attacked some from behind and these fell instantly to the ground with their STUG hanging out.

## CORN-ON-THE-GOD!

Look carefully at these two pictures of a multi-coloured corn god. Are you eagle-eyed enough to spot seven subtle differences?

# English for Beginners

Our next stop is England, a nation of unique individuals and eccentrics, But how did it get that way?
We went in search of the answers by asking..

# London Bridge

Celebrated in song, England's fabled old landmark (AD61-1832) was mainly famous for 'falling down'. Well, after all it had been through, it's not surprising...

## CRAZY RIVER CROSSING

1. Heads of traitors on spikes decorated the bridge. They attracted tourists – and flies.
2. The horrible heads were dipped in tar to protect them from the elements while on show.
3. The bridge was poo central as livestock was driven over it daily, providing regular dollops of goose, horse, and cow dung.
4. Toilet waste was poured into the streets and river, making the lovely Thames an outdoor sewer.
5. This scare-mongering minstrel is singing 'London Bridge is falling down' – a song that could come from the Romans.
6. And being wooden, the bridge was often burning down – and was completely destroyed by fire in 1136.
7. Rat catchers supplied live bait for dire dog-fights, popular with ghoulish gamblers.
8. The river rushed through the arches so fast, sick-minded spectators watched out for sinking boats and drowning crew.
9. Shooting the bridge was a real sport for the batty boatmen but a dip could mean death.

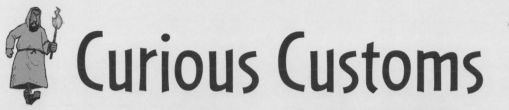

# Curious Customs

English people do some odd things. Like making pancakes or giving away dead deer. Why?

Customs are the funny things that people keep on doing for hundreds of years – sometimes for good reasons, sometimes for no reason. The English are proud of their customs, but after reading this, you may well wonder why...

## Vile Valentine dreams

Girls only. Place a bay leaf under your pillow on Valentine's Night (14 February). You will dream. In the dream you will see who loves you. This may NOT be a good thing, of course.

## Shrove silliness

On Shrove Tuesday (in February) English people eat pancakes and act silly. Curious customs include…

• **Pancake races** – women running down the street and tossing pancakes.

TIPTOE TA –TA!

 • **Tiptoeing** – at Gittisham in Devon the children simply tiptoe from house to house begging. You can pay them if you are daft enough, or tell them to...

## Merrie May baths

In May the weather got warmer. After a winter of wrapping up in thick clothes the Middle Ages English finally threw them off and had a bath. In turn, the man the woman and the babies. By then the water was so dirty you could lose a baby in it! There is an old English saying...

MIND YOU DON'T THROW THE BABY OUT WITH THE BATH WATER!

## June weddings

The people of England usually got married in May or June. Why? Here is a curious answer:

I GOT MARRIED IN JUNE BECAUSE I STILL SMELL QUITE FRESH AFTER MY BATH IN MAY

And the flowers were to mask any leftover putrid pongs.

### DID YOU KNOW?

Hundreds of years ago in Dewsbury, Yorkshire, a man called Thomas de Soothill killed a servant. He was so sorry that he ordered a bell to be made for the local church, and made them promise they would ring it on Christmas Eve to remind him of his evil deed. It is still rung today, once for every year since Jesus was born and once to frighten away the devil. Well, that's him tolled...

# DEAD DEER DAYS

Twice a year (late July and December) the king or queen give four dead deer to the Lord Mayor of London. Why?

It all started with Dick Whittington – and if you haven't heard his story go to the pantomime some time. Mayor Whittington was a rich bloke who loaned King Henry V some money to fight in France (the Hundred Years War).

Henry V won a great victory at the Battle of Agincourt, then came home...

YOU KNOW THAT MONEY I OWE YOU, WHITTINGTON

FORGET IT, YOUR MAJ

YOU WHAT?

YEAH! THE ENGLISH BOYS DONE WELL. TAKE THE MONEY AS A GIFT

YOU HAVE TO LET ME GIVE YOU SOME SORT OF PAYMENT

TELL YOU WHAT. GIVE ME FOUR DEER FOR CHRISTMAS DINNER, EH?

FINE. AND FOUR IN SUMMER TOO IF YOU LIKE. IT'S A DEAL

NO PROBS, YOUR MAJ

And the deer-donating has gone on ever since!

## Blackberry hell

English men, women and children should pick blackberries only on 10 October. According to some, the devil was thrown out of heaven by St Michael and landed in a blackberry bush. As a result, the devil spits on all blackberries – except on this day, which is St Michael's day.

THANKS, I REALLY WANTED TO KNOW THAT

## Grim gurning

Every year since 1267 there has been a fair at Egremont in Cumbria – on the third Sunday in September. Weirdest of all the entertainments is the 'gurning' contest.

To take part you put your head through a horse collar and pull as ugly a face as you can. The ugliest wins a prize. Try this game at school...

'MORNING BOYS

NO GOOD. OUR HISTORY TEACHER WOULD WIN EVERY TIME

## Horrible Halloween

On Halloween many children enjoy dressing up and pretending to be ghosts who have slipped through the 'curtain' from the world of the dead. The Celtic people of ancient Britain held a feast to celebrate the end of summer. The Romans said that the Celtic priests (the Druids) made human sacrifices to the gods at the celebration. They claimed the Druids put prisoners in a huge wooden cage then set fire to it. It's a horrible story, but it might not be true, as the Romans were always making things up about their enemies.

WE ALWAYS HAVE ROAST CHESTNUTS ON HALLOWEEN

WONDER WHAT THOSE DRUIDS ROAST?

# Spooky Pluckley

England is famous for its ghosts, and Pluckley in Kent is even in the Guinness Book of Records as the most haunted village of all!

# NEIGHBOURS FROM HELL

1. WATERCRESS WOMAN This old gin-drinking cress gatherer fell asleep smoking and turned into a flaming fireball – which goes to show that smoking isn't good for you.
2. CREEPY COLONEL Often seen hanging around Park Wood – even after the wood was dug up in 1965. These old colonels can be pretty stuck in their ways.
3. FRIGHT WOODS Just don't go there!
4. HANGING MASTER The ghost of a teacher who hanged himself haunts Dicky Buss's Lane.
5. HORRIBLE HIGHWAYMAN This robber hid in a hollow tree, jumping out on passers-by. One have-a-go hero heard of this and plunged his sword into it. Now the highwayman's ghost haunts the spot.
6. DERING DAME A scary spook that looks out of the Dering Arms window.
7. COACH AND HORSES Every self-respecting ghost town should have one!
8. THE WHITE LADY Lovely Lady Dering was sealed in three coffins when she died, but it didn't stop her coming back.
9. PHANTOM POOCH This paranormal pup must like churchyard bones!
10. DEVIL'S BUSH If you chant the secret phrase the devil will appear!
11. THE RED LADY Another churchyard chimera.
12. POTTY POLTERGEIST The Black Horse pub plays host to an angry spook.
13. SCREAMING MAN He fell into a pit. Too late to cry about it now.
14. MAD MONK A typical English terror who has made Pluckley his home.

# Middle Ages Mind-Benders

## May Day Mayhem

May Day was traditionally one of the maddest celebrations of old England, where the English sang, danced and made merry on village greens and common land. There are five festive differences between the two scenes of Middle Ages may-hem below. Can you spot them all?

## Middle Ages Master Mind

Test your brain with this early English history quiz.

**1. 1066** The nasty Normans arrive. 1,500,000 English are ruled by just 20,000 Normans. The King owns all the land and shares it out among his barons.

**What happened to the English workers?**
A. They became peasants
B. They rebelled
C. They fled to France

**2. 1264** Uppity baron Simon de Montfort wages war on King Henry III. De Montfort is killed, but that's not the end of him. The tetchy troublemaker set up a 'parliament' where the people get to tell the king what to do. It's still around 740 years later.
**What does 'parliament' mean in French?**
A. A place for talking
B. A place where people go to lament their woes
C. A place where you meet your friends

## A-Maze-ing Fun

Hampton Court is one of England's best-known haunted houses. As well as being famous for its ghosts, it's famous for its maze. Imagine you were being chased by a ghost. How quickly could you find your way through?

**To play** Place your pencil on the opening at the bottom, then see how fast you can get to the centre. If you fail, the ghost gets you!

# Dynasty Nasties

Time now to take our historical journey eastwards to China for a terrible tale of fierce families, wars, walls and Asian invasions!

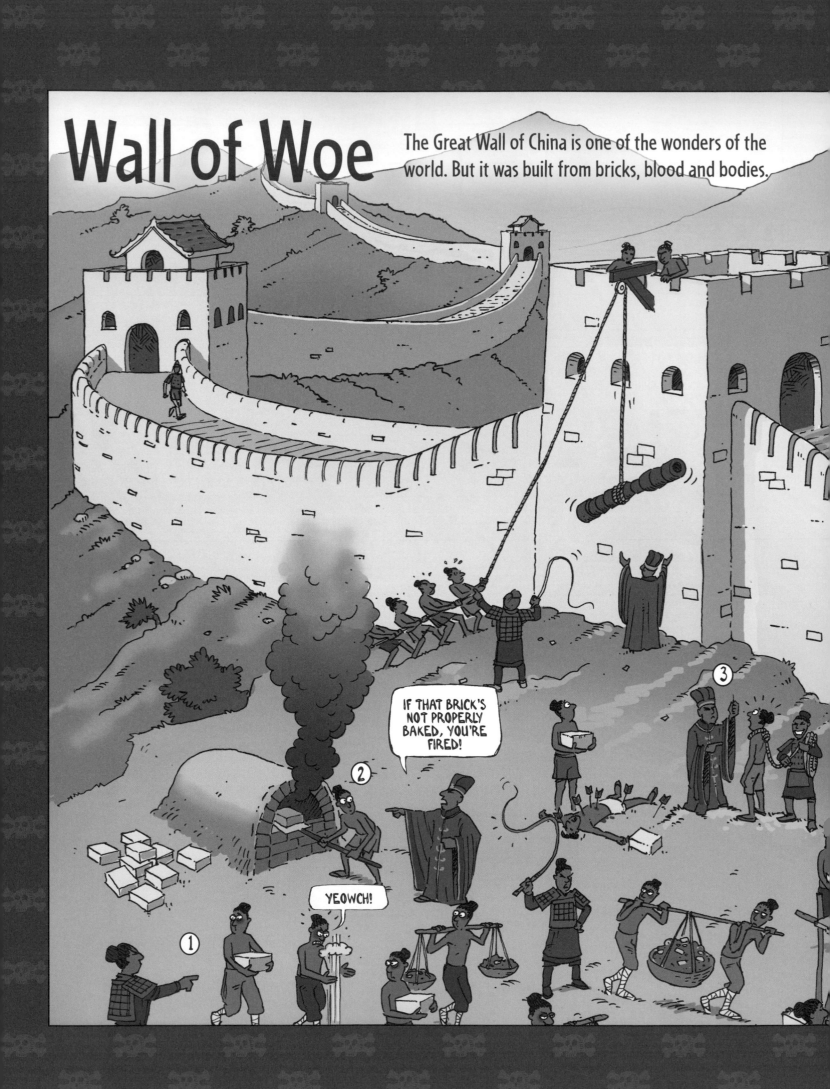

# Foul Foundations

1. For hundreds of years, the Chinese had built walls to keep out foreigners, but the Ming emperors decided they weren't enough. They had all the old walls rebuilt into one big one - the Great Wall of China. This 4160 km-long wall was built from millions of tons of stone – which had to be carried by millions of not-very willing peasants.

2. The bricks for the top of the wall were baked nearby. The bosses were more bothered about making enough bricks than feeding the workers – so many brickies died from hunger.

3. Soldiers and officials kept a close eye on the workers. If a nail could be poked between two blocks, the worker who laid them would get hung. (That way he wouldn't do it again!)

4. The wall was defended by huge cannons – and soldiers with deadly crossbows.

5. Guards used dogs to sniff out intruders –  and as an emergency food when supplies were low. Pot poodle, anyone?

6. The top of the wall was wide enough for horsemen to ride along it. Unfortunately there weren't any 'Men at Work!' signs…

7. The middle of the wall was filled in with dirt and rubble. Workers who died while working were thrown into the wall with the rest of the rubbish – they really put their all into it! No wonder the Chinese call the wall 'The Longest Graveyard on Earth'.

# Painful Punishments

Criminals weren't sentenced to prison – they were sentenced to suffering.
Lots of it. And the punishments could really be a pain in the bottom!

**P**unishment in China wasn't about going to jail. That was just a place to keep prisoners while they were waiting for their trial. No, it was all about pain and public shame. (It still is!) If it hurt horribly or was more embarrassing than your dad's dance moves, then it was used as a punishment.

## Raw bum deal

The people who decided what punishments people should get were local officials. They had more rules than school. The usual punishment for small wrong-doings was being beaten with a split bamboo cane on the bum.

When does 20 mean 16? When it's the number of slaps that were dished out to bottoms. The criminal was let off every fifth blow. This was called the 'grace of the emperor'. Nice chap.

Getting 20 blows or less was just a bit of a telling off.

After the beating, the criminal was expected to bow three times to the judge and thank him for bothering!

THANKS FOR GETTING TO THE BOTTOM OF THINGS

THAT'S ALL YOU'RE CUTTING!

'STOCK' IT – IT HURTS!

Finger stocks were a favourite way of making a criminal confess to a crime. It felt like catching all your fingers in the door at once.

Some serious offenders were punished with three months wearing head stocks. These heavy horrors stopped the victim seeing his feet or reaching his mouth so that he couldn't walk, eat or drink without help. When you were freed you would be caned, branded on the cheek or have your nose sliced off.

Some criminals were branded with a Chinese 'character' letter showing their crime. Getting a nasty letter has never been so unpleasant!

## MING THE MERCILESS

In the time of the mean Ming dynasty, mass floggings were regularly dished out to people who irritated the emperor. Once, 146 government workers or 'civil servants' were flogged so badly that 11 of them died. Not very civil of them, was it?

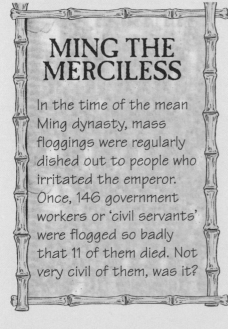

36

WILL THIS DO?

A light punishment was having your beard and 'tache shaved off. It was embarrassing because the only men who didn't have facial hair were eunuchs.

I'VE BEEN WAISTED

Death sentences were usually carried out by beheading – or by chopping the victim in two at the waist.

Top officials or 'mandarins' (no, they weren't orange) decided which cane to use and how many blows to dish out for each crime. They got these rules from a book called 'The Dignity of the Buttocks'! Now that was a book that could really keep you glued to your seat.

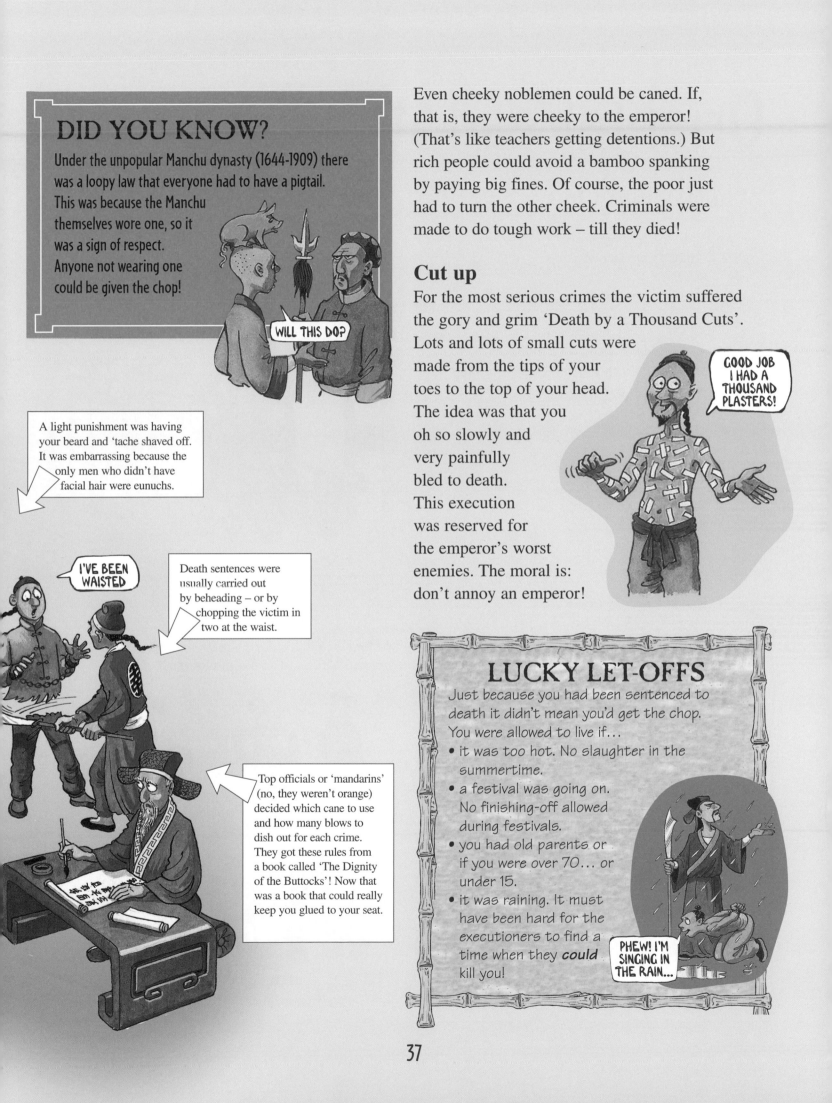

Even cheeky noblemen could be caned. If, that is, they were cheeky to the emperor! (That's like teachers getting detentions.) But rich people could avoid a bamboo spanking by paying big fines. Of course, the poor just had to turn the other cheek. Criminals were made to do tough work – till they died!

## Cut up

For the most serious crimes the victim suffered the gory and grim 'Death by a Thousand Cuts'. Lots and lots of small cuts were made from the tips of your toes to the top of your head. The idea was that you oh so slowly and very painfully bled to death. This execution was reserved for the emperor's worst enemies. The moral is: don't annoy an emperor!

GOOD JOB I HAD A THOUSAND PLASTERS!

## LUCKY LET-OFFS

Just because you had been sentenced to death it didn't mean you'd get the chop. You were allowed to live if...

- it was too hot. No slaughter in the summertime.
- a festival was going on. No finishing-off allowed during festivals.
- you had old parents or if you were over 70... or under 15.
- it was raining. It must have been hard for the executioners to find a time when they *could* kill you!

PHEW! I'M SINGING IN THE RAIN...

# Oriental 'ead Stretchers

## Quick China Quiz

**1. Which of the following was NOT a Chinese emperor?**
a) Han Deeman
b) Wang Mang
c) Wendi

**2. What happened to the last Chinese emperor after he was pushed out of power?**
a) He was shot
b) He became a gardener
c) He became a crocodile farmer

**3. Which people conquered China in the late 13th century?**
a) The Mongols
b) The Wombles
c) The Normans

## Invention Tension

The cheeky Chinese invented many things we now take for granted. But which of these items were *not* invented by them?

SOAP
SPECTACLES
PAPER
CANNON
COMPASS

## Afterlife Strife

The Chinese believed that you weren't just punished for crimes in your lifetime – you paid for them in the afterlife too! Match the crime with the afterlife punishment.

CRIME

1) Robbery
2) Being disrespectful
3) Not paying your taxes
4) Spreading nasty rumours

PUNISHMENT

a) Tied to a red hot pillar and grilled
b) Thrown into a pot of boiling oil
c) Body ground between two large stones
d) Thrown into a fiery volcano

# Euro-Trashed

The next stop is at the end of the 18th Century and the place is Europe. Let's find out about the continental discontent that got the people going potty!

IN 1789 THE FRENCH CHOPPED OFF THEIR KING'S HEAD AND MADE A NEW GOVERNMENT. WELCOME TO THE AGE OF REVOLUTION...

A BLOKE CALLED NAPOLEON TOOK OVER FRANCE AND TRIED TO CONQUER EUROPE. WHEN THE HOLY ROMAN EMPIRE COLLAPSED, IT LOOKED LIKE EUROPE'S OTHER KINGS AND EMPERORS WERE FOR THE CHOP TOO...

TIME TO HEAD OFF, I THINK

BUT IN 1815 MOST OF THE OLD RULERS OF EUROPE GOT TOGETHER AND GANGED UP ON NAPOLEON. THEY BEAT HIM AT WATERLOO. IT SEEMED LIKE THAT 'REVOLUTION' STUFF WAS FINISHED.

LE DRAT!

THEY THINK IT'S ALL OVER

IT IS NOW

TO CELEBRATE, THE VICTORIOUS KINGS AND EMPERORS GOT TOGETHER AT THE CONGRESS OF VIENNA. HERE THEY SIGNED A TREATY THAT MADE SURE MONARCHS WOULD STAY IN CHARGE. THEY MADE LOUIS XVIII THE KING OF FRANCE – WITHOUT ASKING THE FRENCH, OF COURSE.

YOU'RE THE NEW KING OF FRANCE! CONGRATULATIONS!

CHEERS!

GOSH, ISN'T IT LOVELY TO GET BACK TO THE OLD UNFAIR WAYS!

THE NOBLES OF EUROPE WERE PLEASED AS PUNCH, BUT THE POOR STILL HAD NO LUNCH – AND NO POWER. REBELS STARTED TO PLOT REVOLUTIONS...

OUR RULERS ARE IM-POSTERS

THEY GIVE ME A SHORT FUSE

THEY'LL GET OUR POINT IN THE END

THE FRENCH DECIDED THAT THEIR REPUBLIC WAS IN TOO MUCH OF A MESS. THEY WANTED A PROPER GOVERNMENT AGAIN, SO THEY MADE NAPOLEON BONAPARTE'S NEPHEW, LOUIS NAPOLEON, PRESIDENT – AND LATER CROWNED HIM EMPEROR NAPOLEON III.

WE'D LIKE YOU TO BE OUR NEW EMPEROR NAPOLEON

I THINK I CAN PLAY THAT BONA-PARTE!

MEANWHILE, ACROSS THE REST OF EUROPE THE MANY REBELLIONS WERE BEING CRUSHED. IN FACT, NONE OF THE REVOLUTIONS OF 1848 LASTED. THEY ALL GOT BLASTED.

FREEDOM

SORRY MATE – THE WRITING'S ON THE WALL FOR YOU!

BUT THAT'S NOT TO SAY THEY WERE ALL POINTLESS. IN 1861 A RED-SHIRTED ITALIAN CALLED GARIBALDI DECIDED TO UNITE ITALY. HIS SMALL ARMY CONQUERED ALMOST THE WHOLE COUNTRY.

I DON'T KNOW ABOUT HIS FASHION SENSE, BUT I LOVE HIS BISCUITS!

HE GAVE THE LANDS TO KING VICTOR EMMANUEL II OF PIEDMONT, WHO BECAME THE FIRST KING OF ITALY! WHICH LEADS TO THIS AWFUL ITALIAN JOKE...

HOW DID GARIBALDI KNOW HOW TO WIN?

'COS HE'D READ THE VICTORY MANUAL*!

*VICTOR-E-MMANUEL! GEDDIT?

DON'T GET THE IDEA THAT THE FRENCH HAD FINISHED REVOLTING! WHEN LOUIS NAPOLEON LOST A WAR WITH PRUSSIA, THE PEOPLE OF PARIS GOT SO UPSET THAT THEY REVOLTED AGAIN AND SET UP A 'COMMUNE' WHERE ALL WERE EQUAL. THEY BUILT BARRICADES TO DEFEND THEMSELVES...

GIVE US LIBERTY OR GIVE US DEATH!

ERM – WE'VE RUN OUT OF LIBERTY, SO HERE'S SOME DEATH

BUT AFTER A FEW MONTHS THE FRENCH GOVERNMENT SENT THE ARMY IN TO CRUSH THE COMMUNARDS.

IT WASN'T A TOTAL WASTE. FRANCE STAYED A REPUBLIC AND THINGS GOT A BIT FAIRER THERE. EUROPE WAS PEACEFUL FOR A WHILE – WELL, AT LEAST UNTIL THE NEXT WAR...

I GOT SLAUGHTERED FOR THAT? SO THAT MAKES IT ALL OKAY?

# Suffering Subjects

Life was lousy for the European poor – and the rich rulers didn't seem to care. No wonder the poor got sore.

In the 19th century, the Industrial Revolution brought loads of people into towns and cities to work in the new factories. But rents were high so the factory folk had to live in awfully overcrowded houses. These had filthy water and open sewers – which gave water-loving bacteria the chance to really make themselves at home. And these bacteria caused deadly diseases like cholera. It was a killer. When a nurse called Maria went to a slum house in Paris to deliver a baby, this is what she saw…

*A room where the planks that form the wall are coming apart, through which rats are constantly appearing, rats which come in whenever a door is opened, impudent poor men's rats which climb on the table, carrying away whole hunks of bread, and worry the feet of the sleeping occupants. In this room, six children; the four biggest in a bed, the two smallest in a crate. The man, a costermonger, who has known better days, dead drunk during his wife's labour. The woman, as drunk as her husband, lying on a straw mattress and being plied with drink by a friend of hers. During the delivery, an organ-grinder's monkey is on the roof, piddling through a crack onto the snoring husband's back.*

## Cruel for kids

Kids got a rough deal all across Europe. Children were the ideal employees – small enough to fit where adults couldn't and too small to make trouble. Most important of all they were cheap. There were no laws about children at work, so kids as young as eight or nine worked 12-hour days, six days a week. It was worse than school. Here's a young boy's account of his daily, damp drudgery in a mine…

*I pump out the water in the bottom of the pit. I have to pump fast or the water would cover me. I have been two years at the pump. I am paid 10p a day. No holiday but Sunday. I go down at three, sometimes five in the morning, and come up at six or seven at night.*

## The Ridiculous Rich

It didn't help matters that the rich were totally out of touch. Some of them had some very stupid idea about how to behave!

• **Eat more meat** Wealthy people criticised the poor of Paris for not liking meat. The truth was the poor couldn't afford any! It was like being told "They have no bread", and replying, "So let them eat sausages!"

• **Scent yourself** Parisian shops sold small pistols that fired perfume when you pulled the trigger.

A WOMAN IN PARIS COULD BUY A PISTOL POINT IT AT HER HEAD AND NOT HURT HERSELF

I WOULD POINT IT AT MY HEAD... TEACHER

A bit like a water pistol but more smelly.

I THINK I'VE GOT YOURS DARLING

• **Read in the bath** In Napoleon III's time, there was a newspaper called 'The Naiade' that was made of... rubber! People could read it as they soaked in the bath all day.

HMM – STRETCHES THE TRUTH A BIT

The French revolutionaries of 1830 and 1848 had buddies in the art world called the 'Romantics'. And yes, they were quite soppy. In fact some of the Romantics were bonkers. One poet, Gerard de Nerval, liked to take his pet for a walk in the Tuileries Garden in Paris. Nothing odd about that, is there? Except his pet was a lobster. He said it was no more ridiculous than a dog – and it "knew the secrets of the deep".

Do you know why there aren't any good lobster jokes? Because they keep them all to themselves. They're shellfish like that.

**DAFT DEEDS**

COULD YOU TELL ME THE WAY TO KING'S CRUSTACEAN?

## Lazy by law

Mind you – one of the reasons the well-off were so lazy was that there were laws to stop them getting involved with politics.

These laws could be very strict. A famous actor was arrested in the 1860s when he was seen blowing his nose on a handkerchief that had a picture of Napoleon I on it. (Perhaps he thought it was Napoleon Bogeyparte?)

Daft laws like this made the rich angry with the government too. And when the poor AND the rich are ready to rebel, you know there's going to be trouble!

OI! THAT'S SNOT ALLOWED

# Barricade Chaos

In 1871, the poor of Paris decided to rule themselves . They called themselves Communards and built barriers across the boulevards to keep out the army – but these were broken down in beastly street battles.

## STREET STRIFE

1. The Communards sealed off the streets – but they didn't manage to close all the alleys. Looks like some troops have been sneaky snoops!

2. The barricades were made out of anything the Communards could find – stolen mattresses (2A), upturned taxi cabs (2B) and paving slabs (2C).

3. The rebels' guns were rubbish (3A). They did have a mitrailleuse – a sort of early machine gun that looked like a cannon– but even this was rusty (3B)!

4. Poor Parisians helped the Communards get into hot water (4A)! But the upper crust were so cheesed off with bread strikes that they bashed the rebels with baguettes (4B).

5. There are tunnels under most of Paris. Looks like this trooper has tried to use one – and come up under his general's horse by mistake!

6. Gruesome General Gallifet led his cavalry in the awful attack – from a safe distance of course.

7. The firemen of Paris only had buckets of water to put out the blazes started by the Communards.

8. Once the troops took over they cut the Communards to pieces. Far more people were executed afterwards than died in the fighting.

# Some Riotous Reasoning

## Shooting Gallery

In the revolting rebellions, loads of ragged rulers were in the firing line! But who survived to rule another day and who was scrapped?

1. FERDINAND I

2. LOUIS XVIII

3. POPE PIUS IX

4. FREDERICK WILLIAM IV OF PRUSSIA

5. KING OTTO OF GREECE

## Getaway Gear

When revolutionaries came knocking, Europe's mightiest made for the hills. But which of these mad methods of transport were really used by rulers to escape from rebels?

1. Laundry basket

2. Balloon

3. Aeroplane

4. Steamboat

5. Cannon

# Cape Capers

Let's travel south now, to the dark continent and the terrifying tale of South Africa's past. It's a story of settlers and slavery, greed and gold, fighting and finally freedom!

# Veldt Tips

Life was tough for the Boers on the Veldt (grassland). To survive, they needed faith, make-do medicine – and slaves to do the dirty work!

One thing about the Boers was that they were keen on Christianity. Very keen! Boer families got together twice every day for a bible-reading, a sermon and a bit of a religious sing-along.

The Boers might have been Christian, but some of them came up with their own barmy beliefs…

They had all kinds of rules. Even singing hymns wasn't allowed (that was too much fun!).

### Dop stops fun

You'd be amazed how miserable some people can be. Believe it or not, some Boers thought that their religion wasn't strict enough! So they made their own church – the Doppers.

WE BOERS ARE GOD'S CHOSEN PEOPLE!

GOD CURSED THE AFRICANS FOR THEIR SINS

SO IT'S OKAY FOR US TO KILL THEM AND TAKE THEIR LAND!

GOD SAYS THAT ALL THE RACES SHOULD LIVE SEPARATELY!

THESE BELIEFS ARE REALLY BOER–ING!

## BOER MEDICINE

Got a medical emergency? Why not ask a Boer for medical advice? Our guest doctor is Dr Ruud Help…

Dear Dr Ruud, my hand was been shattered when my gun exploded. What should I do?

Dear Dr Ruud, my dad has cut his leg with his axe, and the wound is going stinky and rotten. Please help!

EASY! GET YOUR SON TO CHOP OFF THE MANGLED FINGERS WITH A HAMMER AND CHISEL, THEN USE SUGAR AND SPIDERWEBS AS A DRESSING

THIS LITTLE PIGGY WENT TO MARKET…

SOUNDS LIKE A NASTY AXE–CIDENT! HEAT UP A GOLD GUINEA COIN THEN PRESS IT TO THE WOUND

YOU'LL BE SOUND AS A POUND IN NO TIME!

WHO'RE YOU CALLING A BOER?

## African woes

The Boers may have made their own lives tough, but they made it even tougher for the Africans. Lots of Boers kept Africans as slaves. The Africans did all the hard, dirty work. And if they rebelled – the punishments were worse...

Disobeying an order could be punished by a whipping, being chained up, or even getting an ear chopped off. If you did something really awful, like trying to run away, things got extra nasty.

Then you could be chained up, or tied to a wheel, have your arms and legs broken, then be roasted to death over a fire. (And you thought sports day was bad.)

Dear Dr Ruud, I'm a Boer grandmother and I'm suffering from horrible lumbago (back pain). What can I do?

Dear Dr Ruud, my daughter is suffering from measles. Sorry to put you on the spot, but we really need your help!

IT'S NOTHING THAT A LITTLE LIZARD GREASE WON'T FIX. RUB YOUR BACK WITH IGUANA FAT AND THE LUMBAGO SHOULD GO AWAY. OUT OF IGUANA FAT? DON'T WORRY, VULTURE FAT WILL DO.

COME HERE, YOU!

ALL YOUR DAUGHTER NEEDS IS A NICE CUP OF TEA ... GOAT-POO TEA, TO BE PRECISE! JUST ONE SIP AND SHE'LL SOON FORGET ALL ABOUT THE MEASLES.

HAVE SOME LOVELY POO TEA!

ER... ACTUALLY MAMMA, I'D RATHER HAVE THE MEASLES...

# South African Head Scratchers

## Diamond Shakedown

Rumour has it that three of your workers are hiding a couple of diamonds each about their persons. As claim holder, you'll want to give them a really good search!

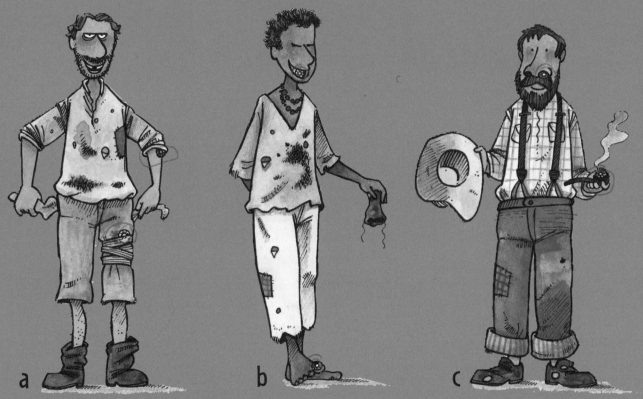

a          b          c

## Double Wagon Worry

The Boers and Zulus are at it again! These two scenes might look the same, but there are six differences. Can you spot them?

# Boom-time Bother

Time to go west for the last stop on our historical tour of the world. Roll up, roll up, and see America grow up! It's a story of bossy barons, bright sparks and businessmen who went off the rails...

WHEN THE CIVIL WAR ENDED IN 1865, MOST OF THE USA WAS IN A RIGHT MESS... AND THE PRESIDENT, LINCOLN, HAD BEEN SHOT DEAD. IT WAS TIME TO SORT THINGS OUT...

WE NEED TO MAKE A NEW, BETTER AMERICA!

WE NEED A NEW PRESIDENT TOO...

SO SETTLERS SPREAD OUT ACROSS THE HUGE AMERICAN WILDERNESS, BUILDING ROADS, FARMS AND MINES. IF INDIANS WERE ALREADY LIVING THERE, THE U.S. ARMY JUST KICKED THEM OUT.

BUT THIS LAND WAS OUR LAND!

WELL NOW IT'S 'MINE'!

WHERE THE SETTLERS WENT, THE RAILWAYS (AMERICANS SAY 'RAILROADS') FOLLOWED. RAILROAD COMPANIES RACED TO BUILD TRACKS ACROSS THE COUNTRY. WHY? WHY DO YOU THINK?

SO THAT'S YOUR LOCO – MOTIVE

WE'RE IN IT FOR THE MONEY!

RAILWAYS WERE GREAT FOR BUSINESS – THEY MADE IT EASY TO GET CROPS AND GOODS TO MARKET. COAL AND STEEL COMPANIES MADE A FORTUNE, BECAUSE THE RAILROADS NEEDED THEIR PRODUCTS. BUSINESS WAS BOOMING!

SOME RICH AND RUTHLESS BUSINESSMEN USED MONEY AND BULLYING TO TAKE OVER SMALLER COMPANIES. THESE BIG BUSINESS BULLIES BECAME KNOWN AS THE 'ROBBER BARONS'.

WE JUST WANT TO KEEP YOUR COMPANY... I MEAN, YOU COMPANY

JOHN D. ROCKEFELLER – OIL BOSS

ANDREW CARNEGIE – RAILROAD CHIEF

I THINK I'M IN BAD COMPANY

SIGN THIS... OR ELSE

J.P. MORGAN – STEEL BOSS

53

# Bloody Bust-up

The USA was the tough kid on the block who lied and bullied its neighbours, but pretended to be goody-goody. (Look out for their six fibs below.)

After killing each other in their very un-Civil War, the Americans were ready to do it to somebody else. They had a good new army and navy and lots of expensive guns that they fancied trying out. They found the perfect opponent – Spain, which still had some colonies in the Americas (like Cuba).

DON'T BE REVOLTING

I'M SICK OF THE REIGN FROM SPAIN

## Pain from Spain

The Cubans were sick of the Spanish and decided to rebel. The US encouraged this because they didn't think anyone (but them) should be a bully in the Americas. Spain sent a huge army to crush the rebels. Some Americans wanted the US to help the Cubans. The Government didn't want to, but the newspapers had other ideas.

## Paper Tiger

Randolph Hearst was a newspaper boss who wanted more readers. One subject that sells papers is a war – but there wasn't one. So Hearst decided to start one! He sent an artist to make pictures of Spain's war and wickedness against Cuba for his paper. When the artist got to Cuba he said nothing was going on. Hearst said...

*You furnish the pictures and I'll furnish the war.*

W.R.HEARST

In other words, you draw some fibs about foul deeds, I'll put them in my paper and THAT will get a war going! That's exactly what happened. (This was American FIB NUMBER ONE.) When the US people saw the nasty pictures they demanded a war against Spain. It looked like Hearst would get his wicked way...

## MAINE MYSTERY

The Yankee warship, USS Maine was on a 'courtesy visit' to Havana. Suddenly the ship blew up, killing most of the crew. What had done it? There were three possibilities...

1. A Spanish mine. (That's what the US said. But there were no Spanish mines there! And Spain had no reason to do it anyway. Fib number two.)
2. It was an accident. (The Maine was a rusty old tub. Its boiler could have just exploded.)
3. The Americans did it (to start war). It probably was an accident. But the papers blamed Spain and wanted revenge. The US President gave in. It was war.

WE'RE SUNK, BUT SO ARE THEY!

It took one more thing to tip America into war...

58

## Sugar daddies

There was another reason for the war: sugar. American companies already owned most of the Cuban sugar industry. They'd wanted to boot out Spain and control the country themselves. But the US had claimed it was 'liberating' Cuba to make it free. That's fib number three.

WE'RE HERE TO SET YOU FREE, SUGAR

SUGAR

HOW SWEET!

The battle at San Juan Hill didn't settle things. But it did scare the puny Spanish navy into making a run for it. Despite stupidly sailing in the wrong direction, the bigger US Navy sank the Spanish armada – without coming to any 'arma' themselves. The war was over. The Americans said that Cuba was now free – free of its Spanish masters – but now run by the the Americans instead! (Fib number four.) Freedom was for US – not them.

# PHILIPPINE FURY

Like Cuba, the US got the the Philippines to rebel against Spain. But when America won the war they just took over from the Spanish. (Fib number five.)

But when Philippine folk fought back, US General Jacob Smith told his troops…

*Kill and burn! And the more you kill and burn the more you will please me!*

Spiteful Smith wanted no more prisoners. He thought anyone over the age of ten could be a rebel and should suffer. The US soldiers killed and burned with the usual excuse…

I WAS JUST FOLLOWING ORDERS

# THE PUTRID PANAMA CANAL

The Panama Canal joins the Atlantic and Pacific oceans. Here's how it got built…

US President Teddy Roosevelt wanted America to get tough with its neighbours. As he put it, "Speak softly and carry a big stick. You'll go far."

MUMBLE MUMBLE MUMBLE

WHAT?

OUCH!

The 'big stick' was the US Navy. The Navy needed a canal at Panama. But Panama was in Columbia – and Columbia didn't want an American canal on their land. So Roosevelt started a revolt in Panama to make it a separate country – and pretended he wasn't doing it! (Fib number six.) This trick worked. Panama let the canal be built.

### CANAL FEVER
Building the canal was woeful work. One worker said, "You get a mouthful of mosquitoes with every breath." Thanks to diseases, about 30,000 men died. That's 3 corpses for every metre of canal.

# ANSWERS

## Warrior Watch page 12

## Wicked Wordsearch page 12
### Hercules and Perseus.

### Questions page 12
1. C
2. B
3. A
(Though athletes that won at the games held in the Greek city of Isthmia did get a celery wreath!)
4. B

## May Day Mayhem page 30

## Furious Fighters page 20
1. True. But not metal armour – it was cotton soaked in salt water to make it hard.
2. True
3. True. They believed precious stones were magic.
4. False
5. True. They often took more.
6. False. They ate enemies but never, ever friends.

## Corn-on-the-god! page 20

## Savage Spanish page 20
ARMS – HEAD – ROLLED – FLOOR – SPEARING – SWORDS – GUTS.

## Middle Ages Master Mind page 30
1. A 2. B
Score 2: you are a Middle Ages Master Mind.
1: you are an Old English Egghead.
0: you are a Medieval moron.

## A-maze-ing fun page 30

## Shooting Gallery page 46

1) Bulls-eye!
2) Miss! Lucky Louis died a king, four years before his brother, Charles X, was booted out.
3) Rebound! Pius had a slice of luck – he ran away when his advisor was murdered, but came back later.
4) Near miss! Fred just survived.
5) Bulls-eye! This German import was forced to flee to Bavaria in 1862.

## Getaway Gear page 46

1) True. It was Prince Metternich who fled Vienna in a laundry wagon.

2) True. The Communard Gambetta escaped Paris in a balloon.

## Double Wagon Worry page 52

## Diamond Shakedown page 52

a) A bandage is always good for a bit of sympathy – and for hiding diamonds. Take a closer look. Don't forget to check out the shirtsleeves too.

b) Teeth and toenails are always good places to look – especially on this native.

c) This Boer might look trustworthy, but look in his pipe and nostril you'll see that he's not.